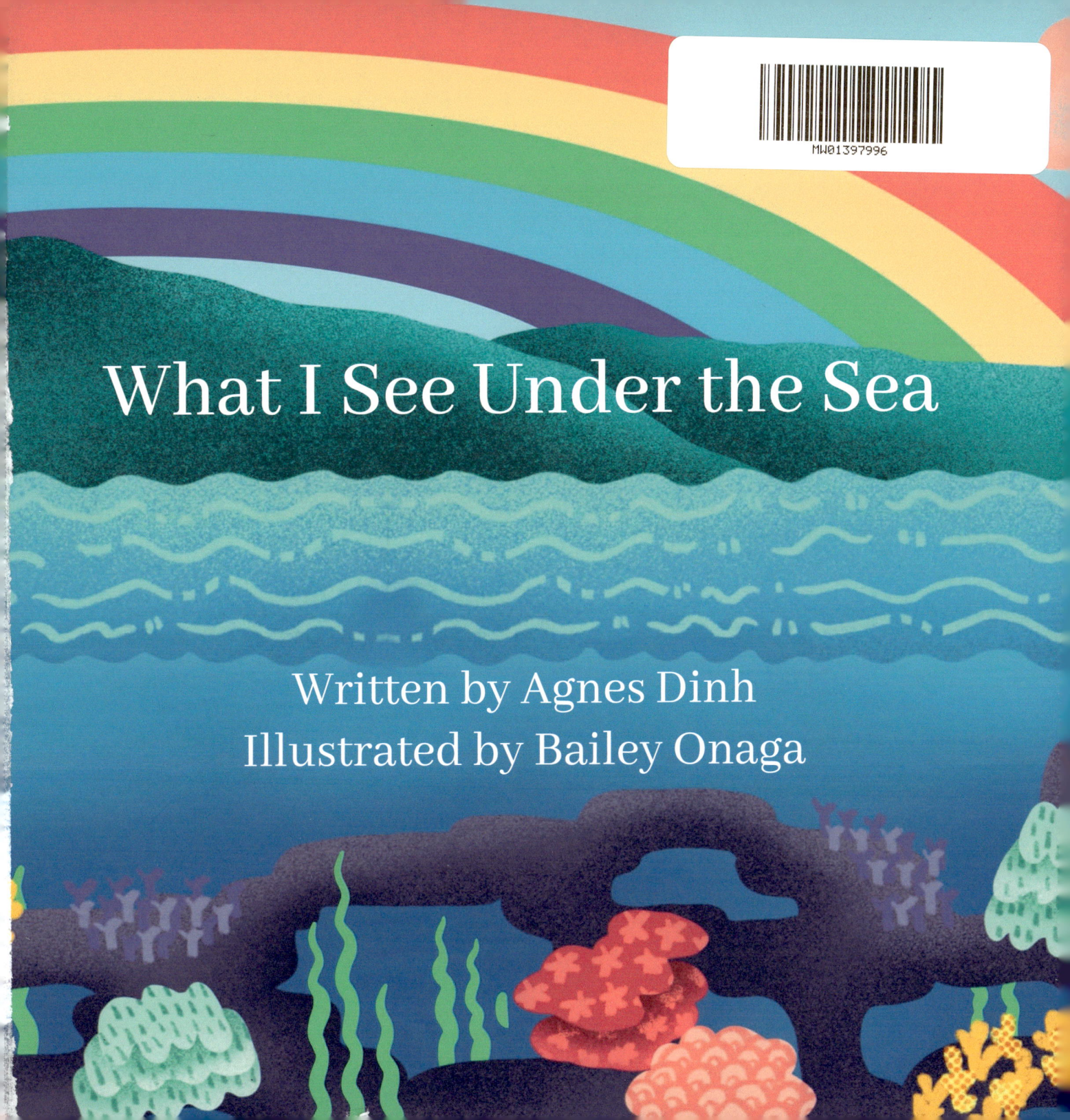

What I See Under the Sea

Written by Agnes Dinh

Illustrated by Bailey Onaga

To Ellie, Ayden, & JJ: Mommy loves you always & forever.
Here's to many more adventures & story time.

To Gary: Thank you for supporting this dream.
On to making the next one come true. Love you.

Copyright © 2023 Agnes Dinh | Ayden's Maui Library LLP
All rights reserved.
ISBN: 9798392955626

Under the sea, I see a jellyfish floating above the reef.

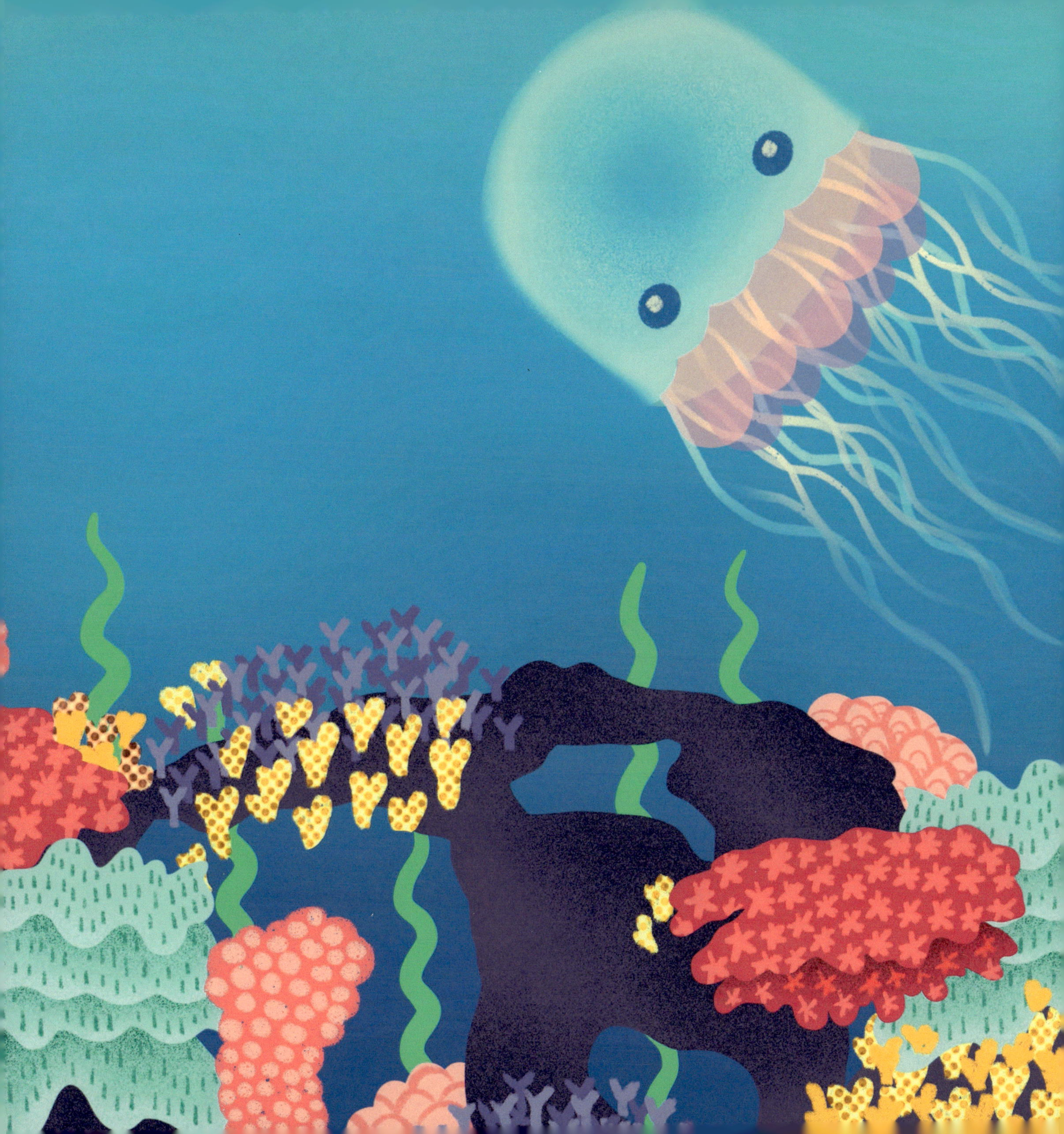

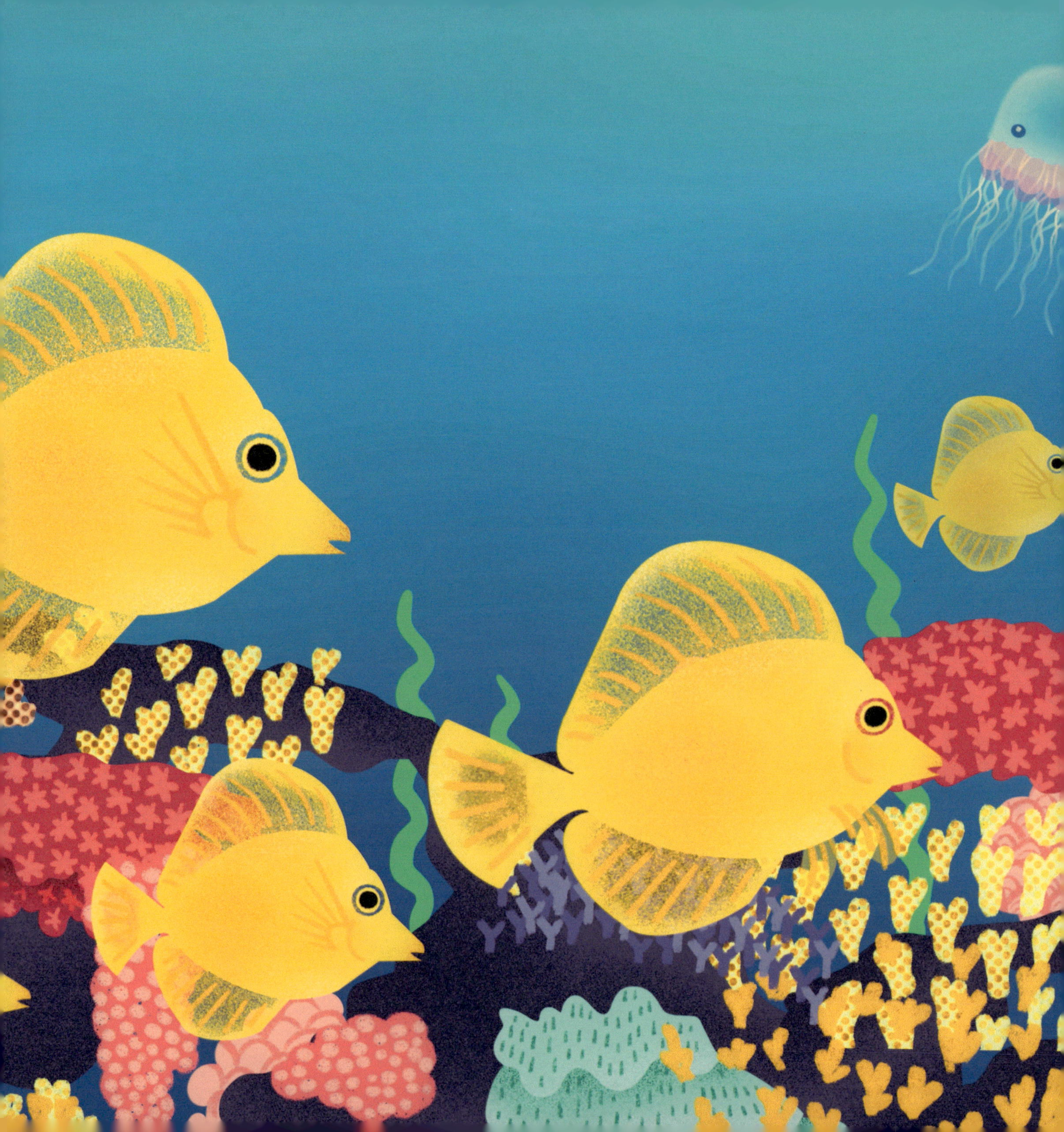

Under the sea, I see a school of yellow tangs swimming with their family.

Under the sea, I see a pufferfish inflating its spiny spikes before me.

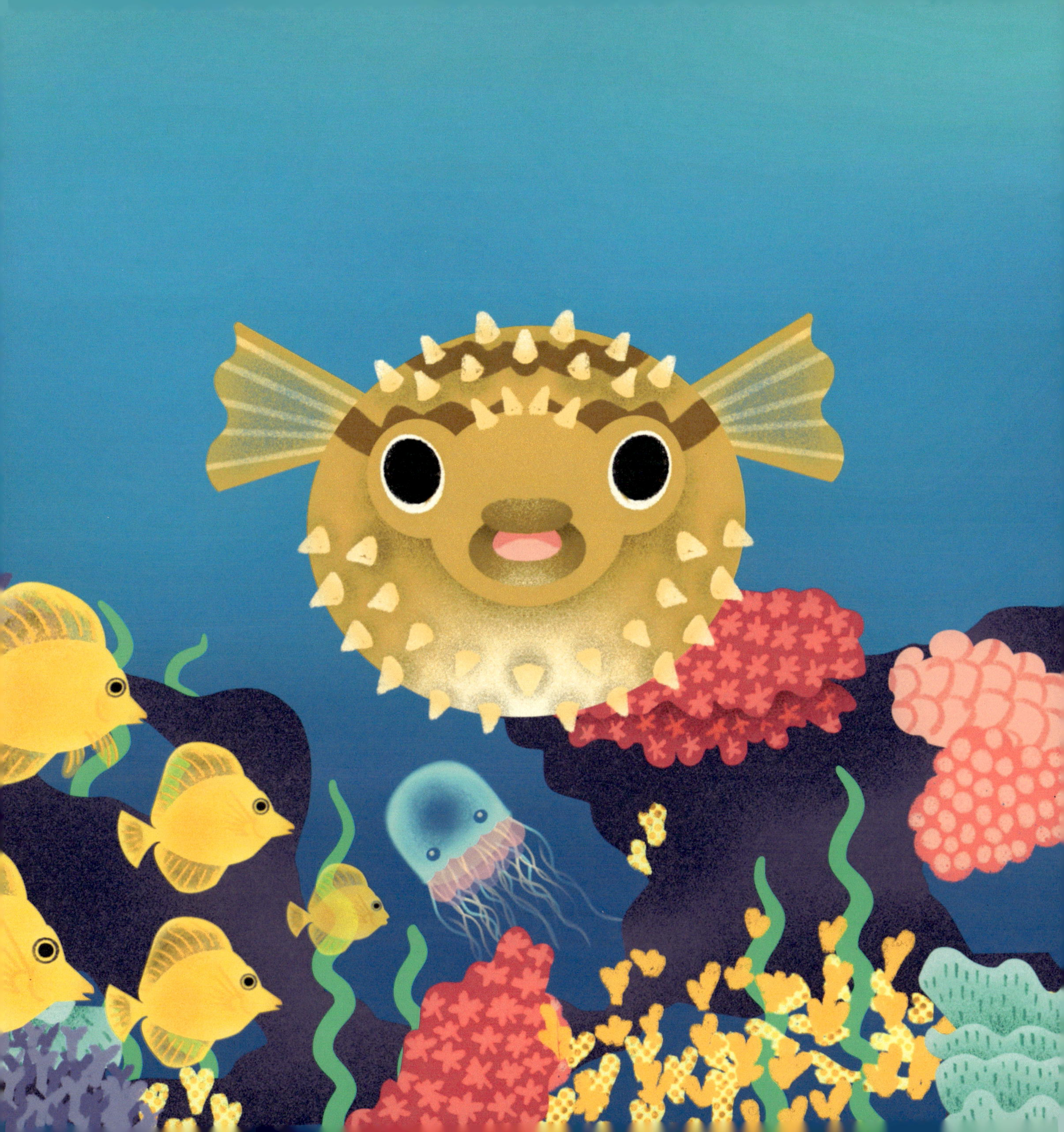

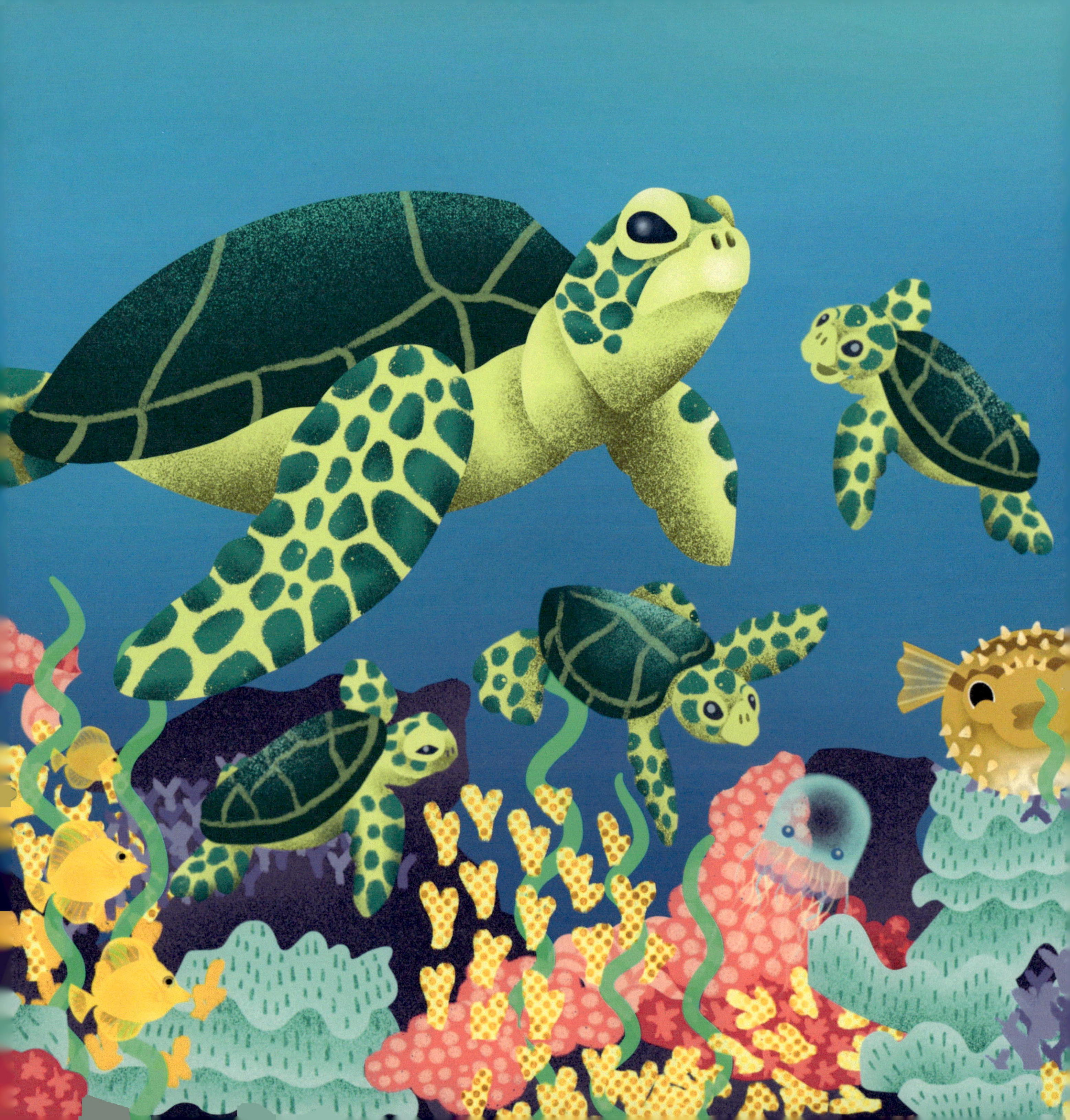

Under the sea, I see turtle hatchlings floating for the first time freely.

Under the sea, I see a triggerfish moving quickly away from divers sneaking a peek.

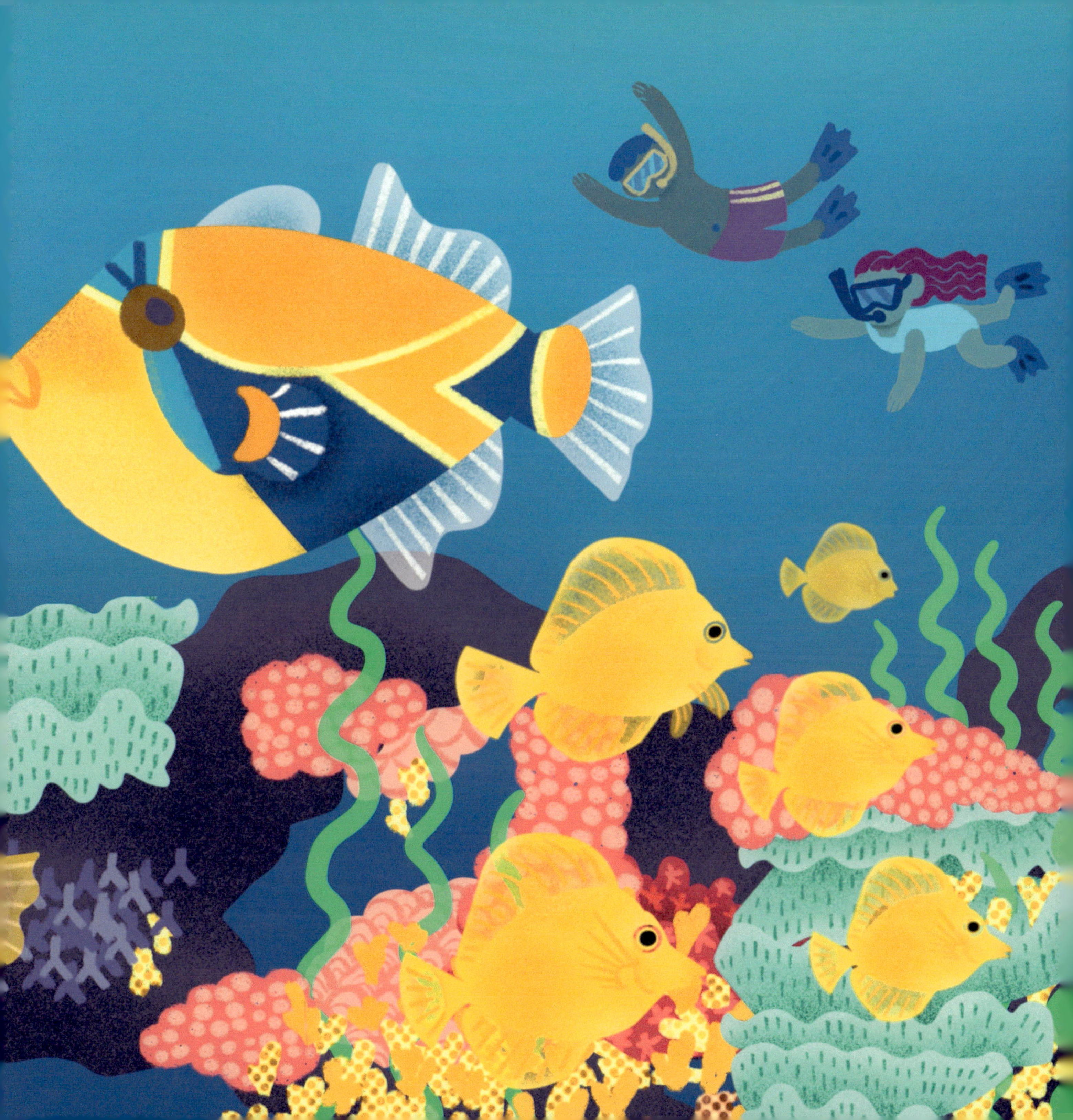

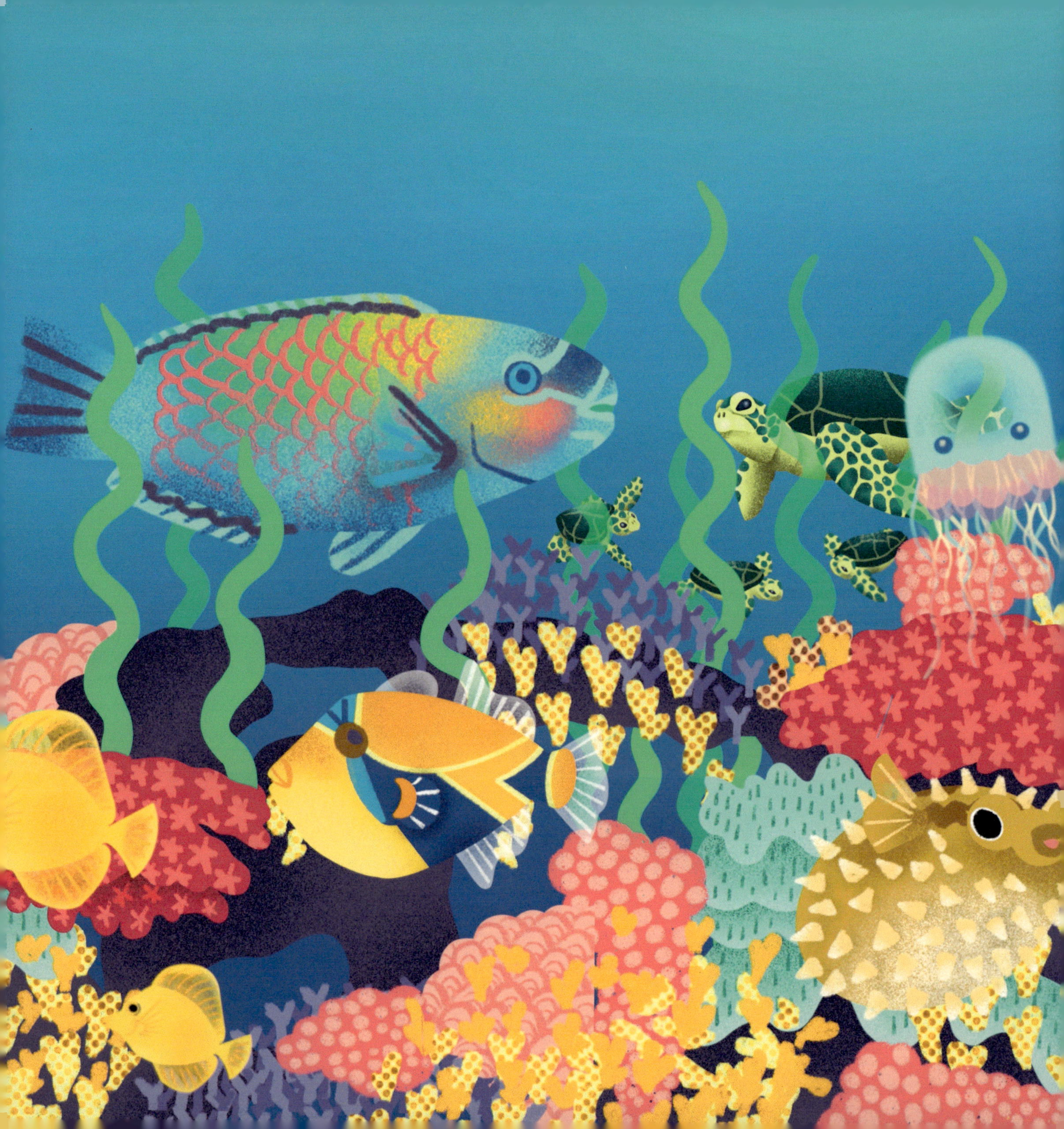

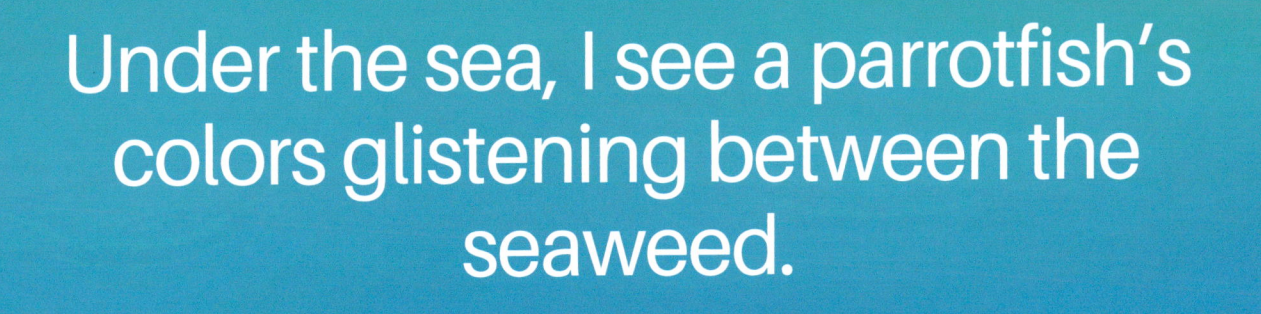

Under the sea, I see a parrotfish's colors glistening between the seaweed.

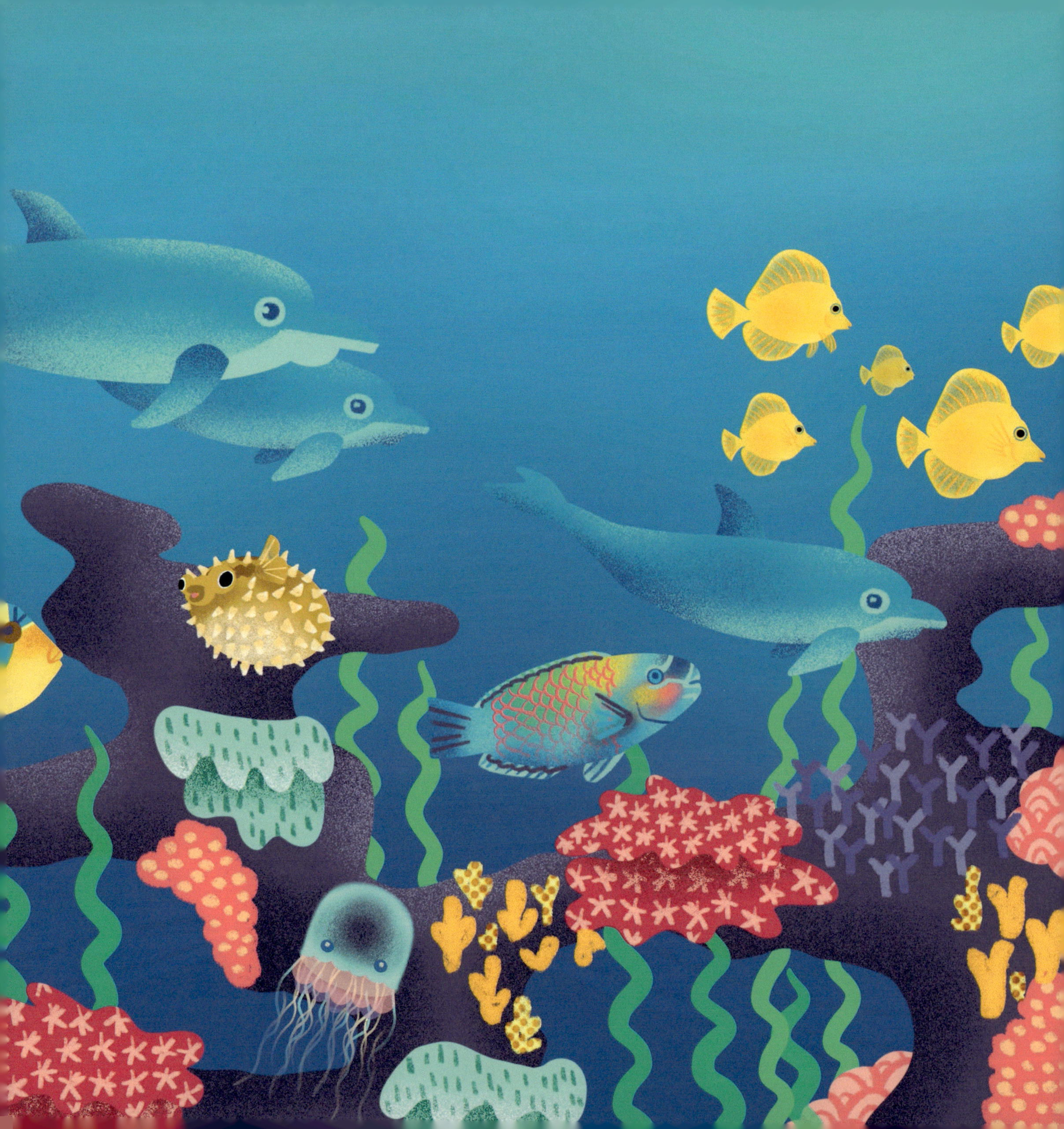

Under the sea, I see a pod of dolphins submerging in the waters gracefully.

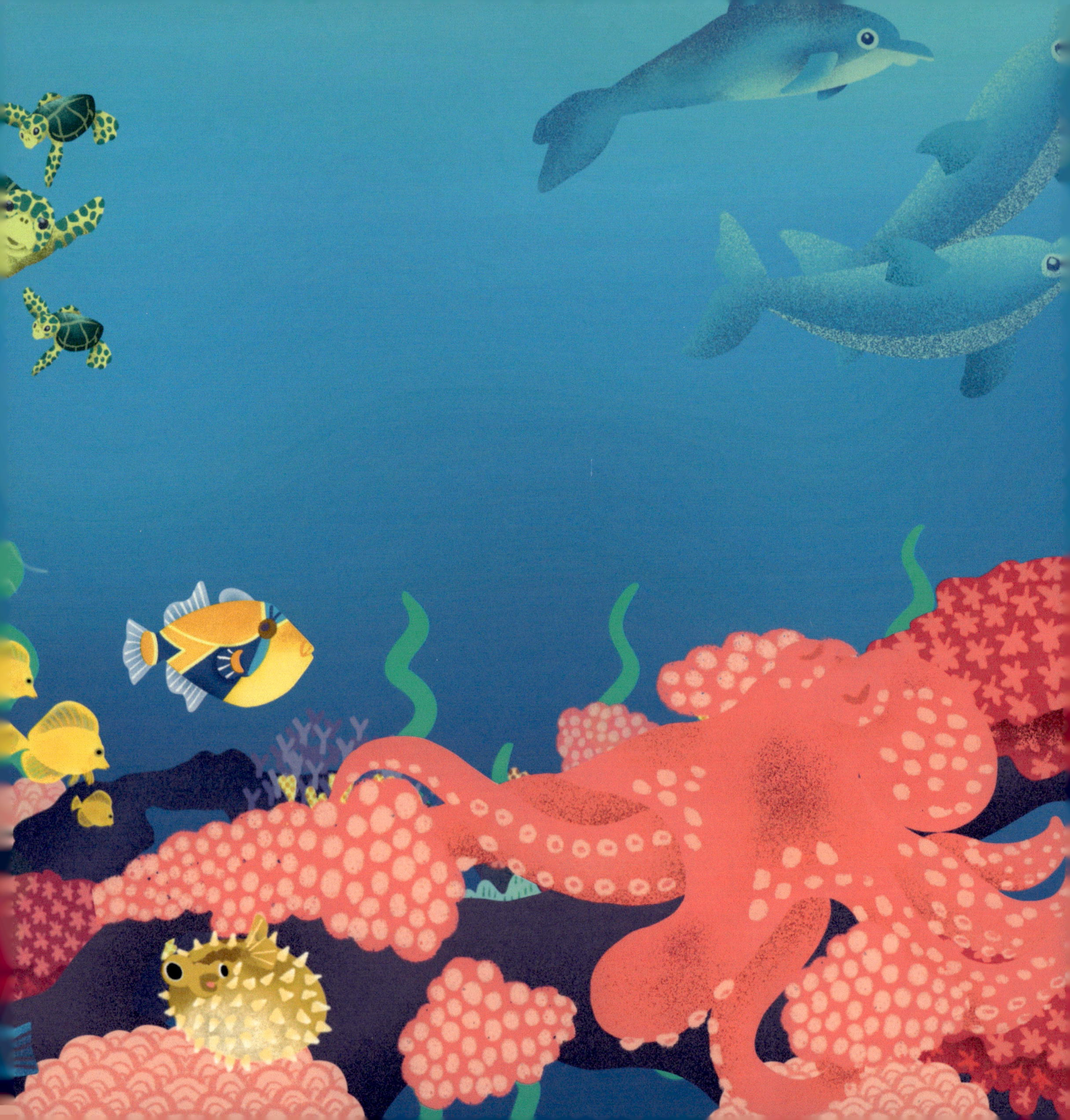

Under the sea, I see an octopus camouflaging with its surroundings.

Under the sea, I see a tiger shark lurking in the reef.

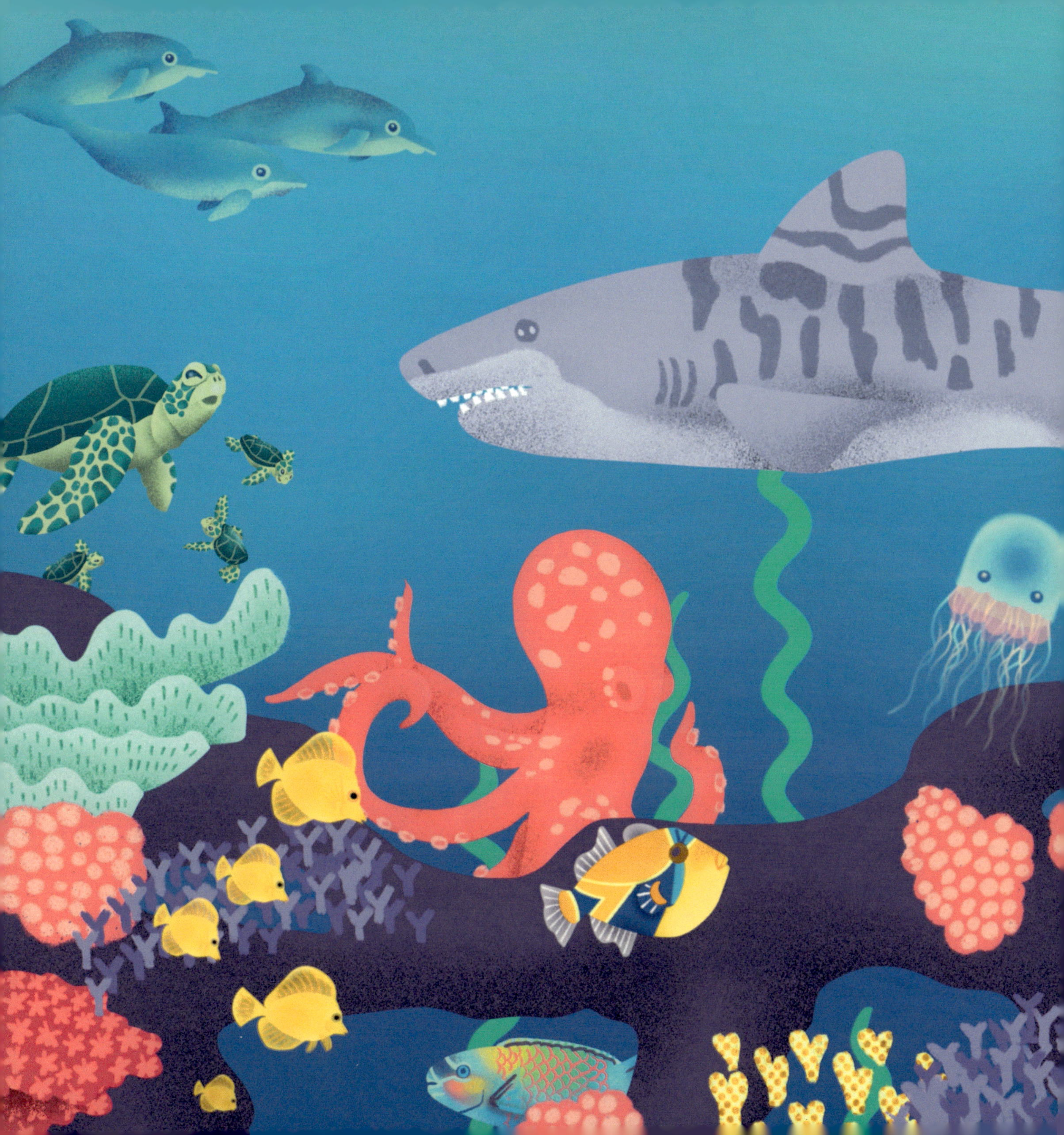

Under the sea, I see a symphony of humpback whales singing and migrating through the warm Pacific breeze.

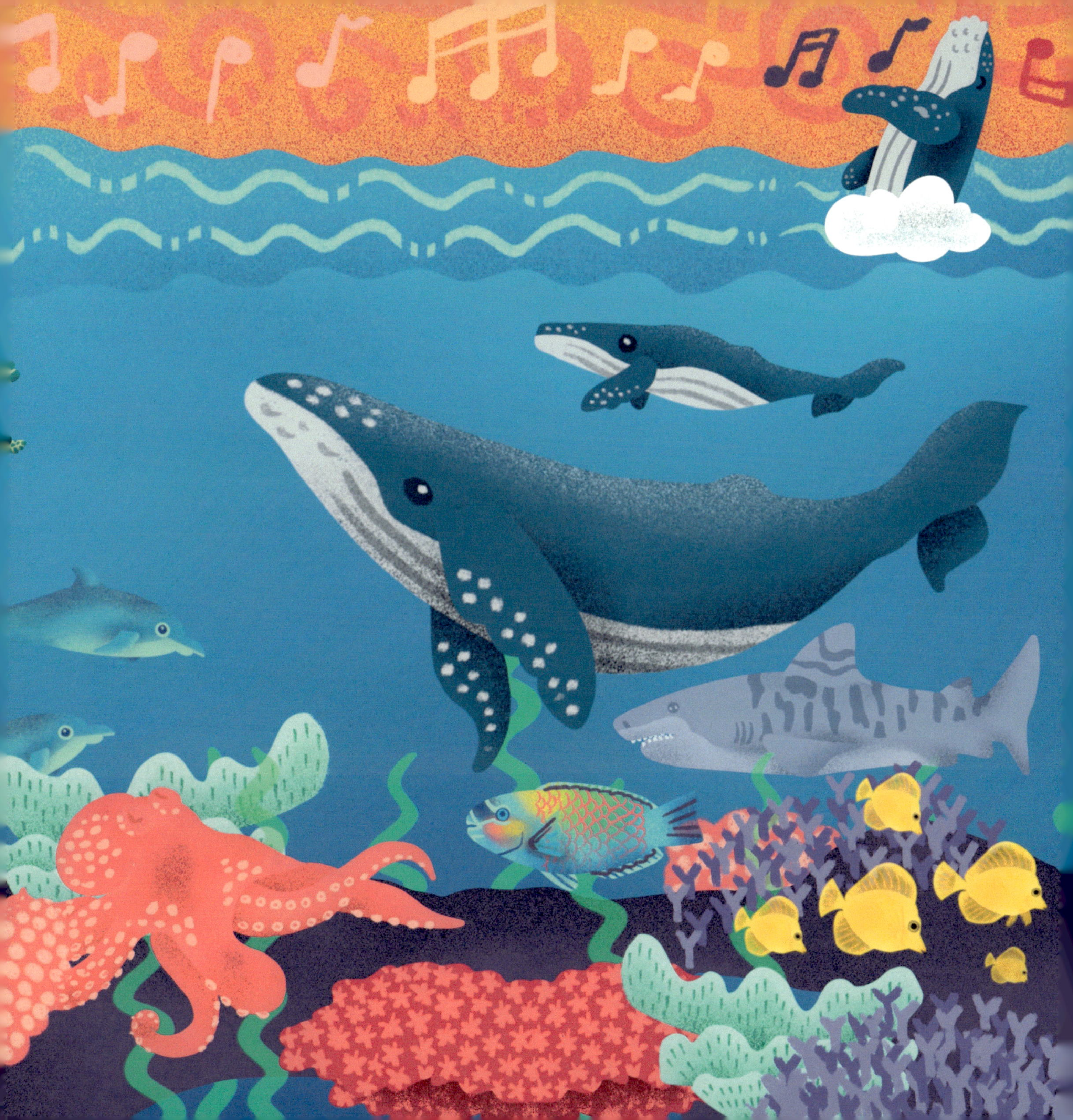

Under the sea,
I see an underwater

world of wonders
just waiting to be seen.

But of all the beauties and wonders of the sea,

nothing compares to the beauty I see before me.

About the Writer

Agnes Dinh is a mom of 3 based in Wailuku, Maui. Storytime has been an integral part of her children's lives. Bedtime routines are never complete without at least 3 stories each night. This, along with her passion for reading and writing, brought on her desire to share story time with other families.

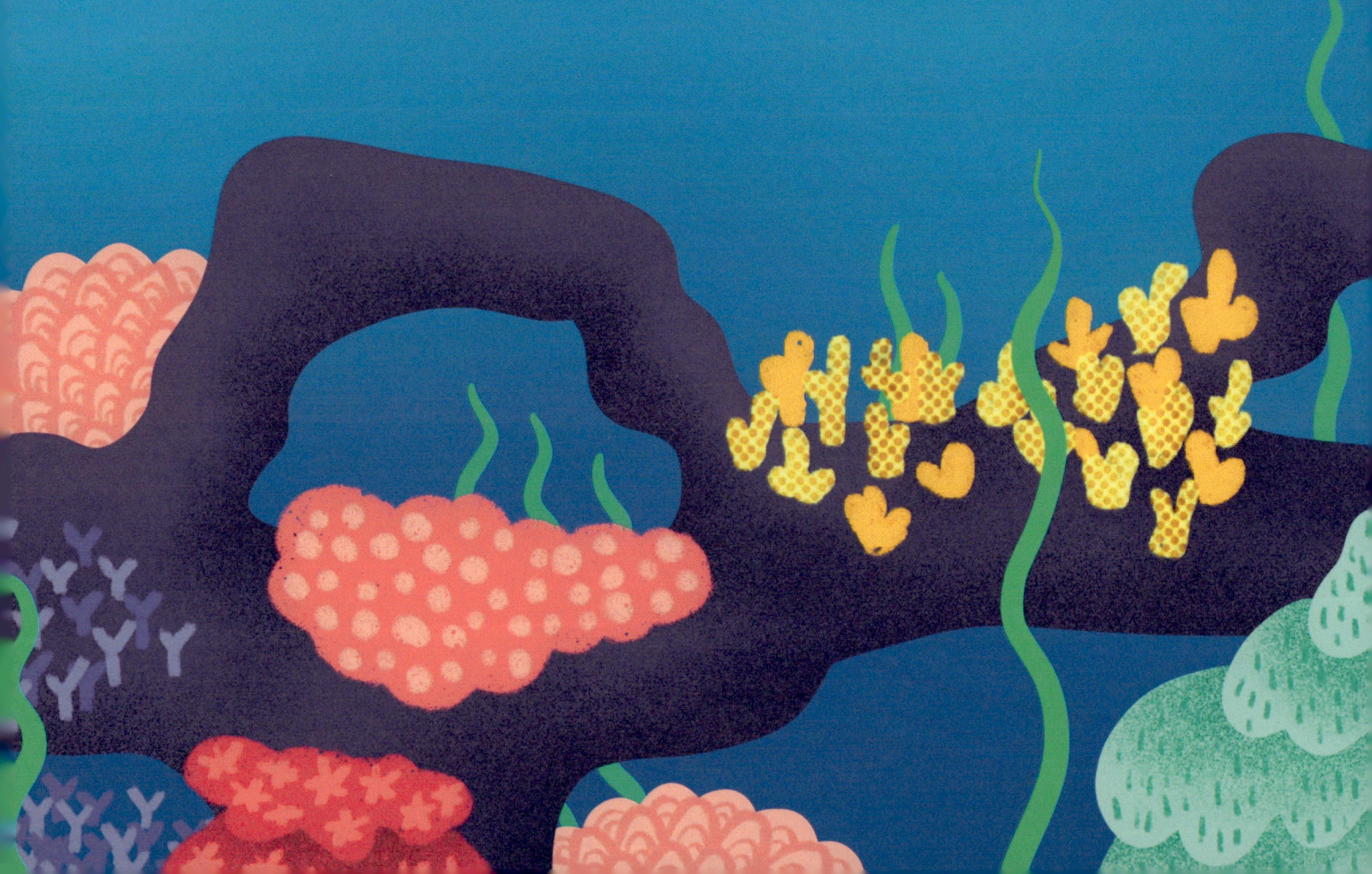

About the Illustrator

Bailey Onaga is an artist born, raised, and based in Wailuku, Maui. Her aesthetic is a homage to her native Hawaiian heritage and 6 years of living in Fukuoka, Japan. She has experience painting murals with Precita Eyes Muralists in San Francisco, where she graduated Summa Cum Laude with a Bachelors of Fine Arts and Japanese Studies. She has also collaborated on installations with her teacher, Philip Sabado. Her art has been exhibited in Hawai'i, Indonesia, and Japan.